# Lagotto Ro₁

The Lagotto Romagnolo is a medium-sized purebred from Italy. Its name translates to 'lake dog from Romagna', Romagna being a region in Italy. It was bred to be a hunting dog, specifically a water retriever so it would bring birds downed or injured from the water to the hunters. Today though it is a great hunter of truffles, the only dog breed used for this purpose and treasured in Italy. As well as being a truffle hunter it is also good at tracking events, rally, conformation and agility. It is also a great companion dog and works well as a therapy dog for people with disabilities and those who are autistic.

# Lagotto Romagnolo Dog

## *Lagotto Romagnolo Information & Dog Breed Facts*

### DEDICATION

# Contents

# History

The Lagotto Romagnolo is thought to be one of the oldest of all the water dogs. They originate from the Romagna region of North-East Italy and Lagotto translates from the local dialect as 'Duck Dog'.

They are thought to have been around for over one thousand years. They were used by locals of the region to hunt for waterfowl in the vast marshlands that covered much of the region in days gone by. Their size, agility, eagerness to please and water-resistant coat meant they were perfectly suited to this task.

The nineteenth-century saw the large scale draining of much of the marshlands in the region. This meant the dogs were no longer required for the work they were used to. Their adaptability meant that they continued to be popular as a working breed, though, and they were developed for their skills as truffle hunters in the region.

During this time, they were often crossed with other breeds known for their hunting and scenting skills, and it meant that the population of pure breed Lagotto dwindled. So much so, that, by the 1970s, they became almost extinct.

Since then, enthusiasts of the breed have worked hard to increase their numbers and to hone their skills as truffle searchers.

They are also becoming increasingly popular as an adaptable and relatively laid back companion breed. They are not as busy as some of their other working counterparts. Demand for the breed is increasing in other countries, and in 2015 they were recognized by the American Kennel Club.

# Care

The Lagotto Romagnolo is an intelligent working breed, and they do need to be kept well-exercised and properly enriched around the house. That being said, they are not as busy as some other working breeds. They can be a little more laid-back around the home, and this can make them appealing even for those living in an apartment.

When outside, be prepared for them having a great love of water. Swimming can be a great way to help them burn off some steam, and don't be surprised if you find it hard to get them out of a river or pond once they have discovered it. Their water-repellant double coat and purpose-built body shape are all geared towards them spending a lot of time in the water.

Because they have been developed for their truffle hunting skills, they also have strong scenting abilities and often a great love of digging. You may need to put extra work in to ensure that they do not start digging up things in the garden that you don't want them to. Some Lagotto owners provide a dedicated sandpit and take part in scent trials and nose work games to give them an outlet for this desire.

Lagottos are known for sometimes being rather vocal; they can be keen alert barkers. You may have to spend some time working on training to ensure that this does not become out of control.

They are a very bright breed though and are keen to please their owner. They respond well to positive reinforcement training methods. With appropriate early socialization and ongoing training, they can be very adaptable, affectionate and happy dogs. They often fit in well to a family environment and can live well alongside other pets.

The Lagotto can also be a good choice for individuals that may suffer from dog hair allergies. No dog is truly hypoallergenic; it is often the dander on the skin that can cause a problem. The Lagotto, however, doesn't really shed, so this means you will not have a hair-filled home. Their coat does need to be groomed out regularly, though, to prevent it from becoming matted, tangled and uncomfortable.

Their ears are hairier than some breeds to help prevent them from becoming waterlogged. The hairs, however, can sometimes become overgrown and cause a build-up of wax and debris. They may need to have excess hair removed to prevent this problem.

Care should also be taken if you are trimming their nails. They are naturally longer and more curved than some breeds. This is to help them with their truffle digging abilities. It means the quick (the blood vessel inside the nail) is longer than average, and you don't want to cut into this accidentally. Not only will you have to stop the bleeding, but it will be painful and could cause your dog to develop an aversion towards nail trimming. You may have to go back to basics with getting them used to the activity.

# Caring for The Lagotto Romagnolo

As with any other breed, Lagottos need to be groomed on a regular basis to make sure their coats and skin are kept in top condition. They also need to be given regular daily exercise to ensure they remain fit and healthy. On top of this, dogs need to be fed good quality food that meets all their nutritional needs throughout their lives.

## Caring for a Lagotto Romagnolo puppy

Lagotto puppies are boisterous and full of life which means it's essential for homes and gardens to be puppy-proofed well in advance of their arrival. A responsible breeder would have well socialised their puppies which always leads to more outgoing, confident and friendly dogs right from the word go. With this said, any puppy is going to feel vulnerable when they leave their mother and littermates which must be taken into account. The longer a puppy can remain with their mother, the better although it should never be for too long either.

It's best to pick a puppy up when people are going to be around for the first week or, so which is the time needed for a puppy to settle in. Puppy-proofing the home and garden means putting away any tools and other implements that a boisterous puppy might injure themselves on. Electric wires and cables must be put out of their reach because puppies love chewing on things. Toxic plants should be removed from flowerbeds and the home too.

Puppies need to sleep a lot to grow and develop as they should which means setting up a quiet area that's not too out of the way means they can retreat to it when they want to nap and it's important not to disturb them when they are sleeping. It's also a good idea to keep "playtime" nice and calm inside the house and to save more active activities and games for outside in the garden which means puppies quickly learn to be less boisterous when they are inside.

The documentation a breeder provides for a puppy must have all the details of their worming date and the product used as well as the information relating to their microchip. It is essential for puppies to be wormed again keeping to a schedule which is as follows:

- Puppies should be wormed at 6 months old

- They need to be wormed again when they are 8 months old

- Puppies should be wormed when they are 10 months old

- They need to be wormed when they are 12 months old

- Things you'll need for your puppy

There are certain items that new owners need to already have in the home prior to bringing a new puppy home. It's often a good idea to restrict how much space a puppy plays in more especially when you can't keep an eye on what they get up to bearing in mind that puppies are often quite boisterous which means investing in puppy gates or a large enough playpen that allows a puppy the room to express themselves while keeping them safe too. The items needed are therefore, as follows:

- Good quality puppy or baby gates to fit on doors

- A good well-made playpen that's large enough for a puppy to play in so they can really express themselves as puppies like to do

- Lots of well-made toys which must include good quality chews suitable for puppies to gnaw on, bearing in mind that a puppy will start teething anything from when they are 3 to 8 months old

- Good quality feed and water bowls which ideally should be ceramic rather than plastic or metal

- A grooming glove

- A slicker brush or soft bristle brush

- Dog specific toothpaste and a toothbrush

- Scissors with rounded ends

- Nail clippers

- Puppy shampoo and conditioner which must be specifically formulated for use on dogs

- A well-made dog collar or harness

- A couple of strong dog leads

- A well-made dog bed that's not too small or too big

- A well-made dog crate for use in the car and in the home, that's large enough for a puppy to move around in

- Baby blankets to put in your puppy's crate and in their beds for when they want to nap or go to sleep at night

**Keeping the noise down**

All puppies are sensitive to noise including Lagotto puppies. It's important to keep the noise levels down when a new puppy arrives in the home. TVs and music should not be played too loud which could end up stressing a small puppy out.

## Keeping vet appointments

As previously mentioned, Lagotto puppies would have been given their first vaccinations by the breeders, but they must have their follow up shots which is up to their new owners to organise. The vaccination schedule for puppies is as follows:

- 10 -12 weeks old, bearing in mind that a puppy would not have full protection straight away, but would only be fully protected 2 weeks after they have had their second vaccination

- When it comes to boosters, it's best to discuss these with a vet because there is a lot of debate about whether a dog really needs them after a certain time. However, if a dog ever needed to go into kennels, their vaccinations would need to be fully up to date.

**What about older Lagotto Romagnolos when they reach their senior years?**

Older Lagottos need lots of special care because as they reach their golden years, they are more at risk of developing certain health concerns. Physically, a dog's muzzle may start to go grey, but there will be other noticeable changes too which includes the following:

- Coats become coarser

- A loss of muscle tone

- Lagottos can either become overweight or underweight

- They have reduced strength and stamina

- Older dogs have difficulty regulating their body temperature

- They often develop arthritis

- Immune systems do not work as efficiently as they once did which means dogs are more susceptible to infections

Older dogs change mentally too which means their response time tends to be slower as such they develop the following:

- They respond less to external stimuli due to impaired vision or hearing

- They tend to be a little pickier about their food

- They have a lower pain threshold

- Become intolerant of any change

- Often an older dog can feel disorientated

Living with a Lagotto Romagnolo in their golden years means taking on a few more responsibilities, but these are easily managed and should include looking at their diet, the amount of exercise they are given, how often their dog beds need changing and keeping an eye on the condition of their teeth.

Older Lagottos need to be fed a good quality diet that meets their needs at this stage of their lives all the while keeping a close eye on a dog's weight. A rough feeding guide for older dogs is as follows bearing in mind they should be fed highly digestible food that does not contain any additives:

- Protein content should be anything from 14 – 21%

- Fat content should be less than 10%

- Fibre content should be less than 4%

- Calcium content should be 0.5 – 0.8%

- Phosphorous content should be 0.4 – 0.7

- Sodium content should be 0.2 – 0.4%

Older Lagottos don't need to be given the same amount of daily exercise as a younger dog, but they still need the right amount of physical activity to maintain muscle tone and to prevent a dog from putting on too much weight. All dogs need access to fresh clean water and this is especially true of older dogs when they reach their golden years because they are more at risk of developing kidney disorders.

# Your Pup's Price Tag

A Lagotto puppy will cost about $1800 for a pet quality dog from a trustworthy breeder, or even double that for a show quality dog from a top breeder. Even the former will have to put you on a waiting list as there are only about 500 puppies being registered a year. It would be tempting then to turn to over sources like pet stores, back yard breeders or even puppy mills. However there are a couple of good reasons to avoid doing this. You have no guarantees about the health of your dog and you are funding people who are negligent at best, cruel at worst. Worth mentioning is that checking out rescues and shelters is a great option. While you may not be likely to find a purebred Lagotto you may find a mix or even another dog that you fall in love with, and these dogs are desperate for people to give them another chance at a forever home.

When you have your puppy or dog there are some things you need to have at home like a crate, carrier, collar and leash, bowls and such. These will cost you about $200. Then there are initial medical costs you should have done as soon as you have your puppy. A vet needs to give it a physical exam, do some blood tests, deworm it, spay or neuter it, micro chip it and have its shots up to date. These will cost about $270.

Then there are ongoing annual costs to be sure you are ready for. The basic health care needs of flea and tick prevention, check ups and shots along with pet insurance will be at least $460 a year. Feeding your dog will be around $145 a year for a good quality dry dog food and dog treats. Miscellaneous costs covering needs like licenses, miscellaneous items, toys, grooming and basic training come to about $535 a year. This gives an annual total starting figure of $1140.

# Appearance

Height at the withers: Males 43 - 48 cm, Females 41 - 46 cm at the withers

Average weight: Males 13 - 16 kg, Females 11 - 14 kg

The Lagotto Romagnolo is a handsome dog and one that commands a lot of presence. They are small to medium in size and quite squarely built which gives them a sturdy appearance which is accentuated by a dog's curly, woolly coat. There is a distinct difference between both male and female dogs. Their heads are moderately broad with dogs having slightly convex skulls and slight, but noticeable stops. Eyebrow arches are well developed, and muzzles are strong being almost as deep as they are long. They have straight nasal bridges and large noses that boast well opened nostrils. Their jaws are powerful and large with tight lips and covered in bristly, long whiskers.

They have quite large eyes which are set nicely on a dog's face without being too close. Eye lashes are well developed, and eye colours can range from ochre to a dark hazel as well as brown to match a dog's coat colour. The Lagotto always has an alert, intelligent expression which adds to their endearing looks. Ears are quite large and triangular having rounded tips. They are wider at the base being set just above the level of a dog's eyes. Their ears hang down when relaxed but are slightly raised when a dog is excited or alert.

The Lagotto has a strong jaw and they can either have a scissor or a pincer bite, although a reverse scissor bite is also allowed under their breed standard. Their necks are quite short, but powerful and muscular being slightly arched with no dewlap. Their shoulders are well muscled and quite well laid back. Front legs are powerful and well-muscled showing a good amount of bone.

The Lagotto has a strong compact body with their toplines falling from the wither to the croup. Their backs are muscular with dogs having short, wide and extremely powerful, slightly arched loins and wide, long and sloping croups. Their chests are well developed reaching down to a dog's elbows. Bellies are slightly tucked up adding to a Lagotto's athletic, streamlined appearance.

Their hindquarters are strong, with dogs having powerful upper thighs. Their feet are compact having strong nails and webbing between a dog's toes which is why they are such strong swimmers. A Lagotto's front feet are virtually round with tight, well arched toes whereas their back feet are a little more oval shaped and the toes are not so arched. Tails are set as a continuation of a dog's croup and taper towards the tip hanging down when at rest, but when excited dogs often carry their tails over their backs although never curled.

When it comes to their coat, the Lagotto Romagnolo boasts having an extremely waterproof coat that's woolly and rough to the touch that forms extremely thick curls. Their undercoat is clearly visible being softer and dense. The curls form all over a dog's body, but they are looser on their head which forms their eyebrows, whiskers and beards. A dog's cheeks are nicely covered in thick hair and the curls on their ears are very wavy and open. Inner ear flaps are covered with hair and tails are covered in bristly, woolly hair. The accepted coat colours for Kennel Club registration are as follows:

- Brown
- Brown & White
- Brown Roan
- Off White
- Orange
- Orange & White
- Orange Roan
- White

Dogs can have a brown or dark brown mask which is acceptable under the breed standard.

It is worth noting that the accepted breed colours for Kennel Club registration can differ from those set out in the breed standard which are as follows:

- Solid off-white

- White with orange or brown markings

- Brown roan

- Solid brown (all shades)

- Solid orange

Lagottos can have brown or dark brown masks with pigmentation being anything from light to a very dark brown.

## Gait/movement

When a Lagotto Romagnolo moves, they do so with a smooth, free and tireless action showing plenty of drive from behind.

## Faults

The Kennel Club frowns on any exaggerations or departures from the breed standard and would judge the faults on how much they affect a dog's overall health and wellbeing as well as their ability to perform.

Males should have both testicles fully descended into their scrotums and it is worth noting that a dog can be a little lighter or heavier as well as slightly taller or shorter than set out in the Kennel Club breed standard which is only given as a guideline.

# Temperament

Although the Lagotto is first and foremost a working dog, they do make wonderful family pets providing they are given the right amount of daily exercise and mental stimulation to keep them busy and happy both physically and mentally. They are known to be exceptionally good natured around children and love nothing more than to be part of a family.

They are best suited to people who lead active, outdoor lives and who would like to have an energetic, intelligent canine companion at their side. They are not the best choice for first time owners because they need to be handled and trained by people who are familiar with this type of dog's specific needs. The Lagotto does boast having quite a high prey drive having extremely good hearing as well as a very keen sense of smell. They can also spot their prey in the distance which means that when they are being trained, attention must be paid to the "recall" command right from the word go.

They love being in and around water which means care must be taken as to where and when they can run off their leads just in case a dog decides to jump in any of the more dangerous water courses. They also love to dig which can become a problem if dogs roam around a garden which often sees a Lagotto happily digging up flower beds and lawns.

Lagottos form very strong bonds with their owners and as such they like to be with them and are never happy when left to their own devices for any length of time which could see a dog developing some unwanted and destructive behaviours as a way of relieving their stress. They often suffer separation anxiety when they are left alone for long periods of time.

**Are they a good choice for first time owners?**

Lagottos are a good choice for first time dog owners because they are so amenable and people-oriented, loving nothing more than to please and to entertain their families. They are particularly good with young children and older people too although playtime can get a bit boisterous at times. With this said, anyone sharing a home with a

Lagotto would need to ensure they have the time to dedicate to an intelligent and active, yet sensible little dog.

## What about prey drive?

Although Lagottos are very social by nature, they have working and hunting dogs in their lineage and as such they have a high prey drive. As such, care should always be taken as to where and when a dog can run free more especially when there is livestock or wildlife close by.

## What about playfulness?

Lagottos have a very playful side to their natures and love to entertain and be entertained. They are known to be a little mischievous when the mood takes them and being so clever, they quickly learn what pleases an owner and how to get their own way when they want something.

## What about adaptability?

Lagottos are known to be highly adaptable dogs and providing they are given enough daily physical exercise combined with as much mental stimulation to prevent boredom from setting in they are just as happy living in an apartment in town as they would be living in a house in the country.

## What about separation anxiety?

Lagottos form strong ties with their families and dogs are never very happy when they find themselves left on their own for longer periods of time. They are better suited to people who either work from home or in households where one person stays at home when everyone else is out, so they are never alone for any length of time which could see a dog suffering from separation anxiety. This can lead to them being destructive around the home which is a dog's way of relieving any stress they are feeling and a way to keep themselves entertained.

**What about excessive barking?**

The Lagotto is not known to be a "barker" or yappy little dog even though they have a very acute sense of hearing. With this said, if there are strangers around, a Lagotto can be quite vocal which is why they are such good watchdogs.

**Do Lagotto Romagnolos like water?**

Lagottos adore being water having been bred for centuries to be "water dogs" and they will take to the water whenever they can no matter what the weather. However, if anyone who owns a dog that does not like water should never force them to go in because it would just end up scaring them. With this said, care should always be taken when walking a Lagotto off the lead anywhere near more dangerous watercourses just in case a dog decides to leap in and then needs rescuing because they cannot get out of the water on their own.

## Are Lagotto Romagnolos good watchdogs?

Lagottos are extremely good watchdogs and as previously mentioned, they sleep with one eye and one ear open which in short means if there are strangers about, they are quick to let an owner know something is going on.

# Health

The average life expectancy of a Lagotto Romagnolo is between 15 and 17 years when properly cared for and fed an appropriate good quality diet to suit their ages.

The Lagotto Romagnolo is known to suffer from a few hereditary health issues which are worth knowing about if you are planning share your home with one of these unusual and handsome dogs. The conditions that seem to affect the breed the most include the following:

- Hip dysplasia – dogs should be hip scored through the Animal Health Trust (AHT)

- Elbow dysplasia – dogs should be elbow tested through the Animal Health Trust (AHT)

- Hereditary cataracts – dogs should be eye tested through British Veterinary Association/Kennel Club/International Sheepdog

Society Eye Scheme

- Lysosomal storage disease

- Juvenile epilepsy

- Cerebella anomaly

- Hypothyroidism

- Alopecia

- Short hair/improper coat – test available through OptiGen

**What about vaccinations?**

Lagotto puppies would have been given their initial vaccinations before being sold, but it is up to their new owners to make sure they have their follow-up shots in a timely manner with the vaccination schedule for puppies being as follows:

10 -12 weeks old, bearing in mind that a puppy would not have full protection straight away, but would be fully protected 2 weeks after they have had their second vaccination

There has been a lot of discussion about the need for dogs to have boosters. As such, it's best to talk to a vet before making a final decision on whether a dog should continue to have annual vaccinations which are known as boosters.

**What about spaying and neutering?**

A lot of vets these days recommend waiting until dogs are slightly older before spaying and neutering them which means they are more mature before undergoing the procedures. As such they advise neutering males and spaying females when they are between the ages of 6 to 9 months old and sometimes even when a dog is 12 months old.

Other vets recommend spaying and neutering dogs when they are 6 months old, but never any earlier unless for medical reasons. With this said, many breeds are different, and it is always advisable to discuss things with a vet and then follow their advice on when a dog should be spayed or neutered.

**What about obesity problems?**

Like other breeds, Lagottos can gain weight after they have been spayed or neutered and it's important to keep an eye on a dog's waistline just in case they do. If a dog starts to put on weight, it's important to adjust their daily calorie intake and to up the amount of exercise they are given. Older dogs too are more prone to gaining weight and again it's essential they be fed and exercised accordingly because obesity can shorten a dog's life by several years. The reason being that it puts a lot of extra strain on a dog's internal organs including the heart which could prove fatal.

**What about allergies?**

Some Lagottos are prone to suffering from allergies and it's important for a dog to see a vet sooner rather than later if one flares up. Allergies can be notoriously hard to clear up and finding the triggers can be challenging. With this said, a vet would be able to make a dog with an allergy more comfortable while they try to find out the triggers which could include the following:

Certain dog foods that contain high levels of cereal and grain-type fillers

- Airborne pollens

- Dust mites

- Environment

- Flea and tick bites

- Chemicals found in everyday household cleaning products

- Participating in health schemes

All responsible Lagotto Romagnolo breeders would ensure that their stud dogs are tested for known hereditary and congenital health issues known to affect the breed by using the following schemes:

- DNA test for JE

- BVA/KC hip dysplasia scheme\

- BVA/KC elbow dysplasia scheme

- DNA test for LSD

- Eye testing

**What about breed specific breeding restrictions?**

Apart from the standard breeding restrictions for all Kennel Club recognised breeds, there are no other breed specific breeding restrictions in place for the Lagotto Romagnolo.

**What about Assured Breeder Requirements?**

It is mandatory for all KC Assured Breeders to use the following tests on their dogs and all other breeders are strongly advised to follow suit:

## DNA test for JE

BVA/KC hip dysplasia schemeThe Kennel Club also strongly recommends that all breeders use the following schemes on their dogs:

- BVA/KC elbow dysplasia scheme

- DNA test for LSD

- Eye testing

# Lagotto Romagnolo Buying Advice

When visiting and buying any puppy or dog, there are many important things to consider and questions to ask of the breeder/seller. You can read our generic puppy/dog advice here which includes making sure you see the puppy with its mother and to verify that the dog has been wormed and microchipped.

Lagotto Romagnolo puppies are quite a rare breed in the UK which means that well-bred puppies command a lot of money. As such, with Lagottos there is specific advice, questions and protocols to follow when buying a puppy which are as follows:

- Beware of online scams and how to avoid them. You may see online and other adverts by scammers showing images of beautiful Lagotto Romagnolo puppies for sale at very low prices. However, the sellers ask buyers for money up front before agreeing to deliver a puppy to a new home. Potential buyers should never buy a puppy unseen and should never pay a deposit or any other money online to a seller. You should always visit the pet at the sellers home to confirm they are genuine and make a note of their address.

- As previously touched upon, not many Lagotto Romagnolo puppies are available every year and they are expensive. As such, amateur breeders/people who breed from a dam far too often, so they can make a quick profit without caring for the welfare of the puppies, their dam or the breed in general. Under Kennel Club rules, a dam can only produce 4 litters and she must be between a certain age to do so. Anyone wishing to buy a Lagotto Romagnolo puppy should think very carefully about who they purchase their puppy from and should always ask to see the relevant paperwork pertaining to a puppy's lineage, their vaccinations and their microchipping.

- Prospective owners should be aware that many reputable breeders insist on placing restrictions on puppies when it comes to breeding and exporting them and should explain the restrictions well in advance of selling any puppies.

# Feeding

If you get a Lagotto puppy from a breeder, they would give you a feeding schedule and it's important to stick to the same routine, feeding the same puppy food to avoid any tummy upsets. You can change a puppy's diet, but this needs to be done very gradually always making sure they don't develop any digestive upsets and if they do, it's best to put them back on their original diet and to discuss things with the vet before attempting to change it again.

Older dogs are not known to be fussy eaters, but this does not mean they can be fed a lower quality diet. It's best to feed a mature dog twice a day, once in the morning and then again in the evening, making sure it's good quality food that meets all their nutritional requirements. It's also important that dogs be given the right amount of exercise, so they burn off any excess calories or they might gain too much weight which can lead to all sorts of health issues. Obesity can shorten a dog's life by several years so it's important to keep an eye on their waistline from the word go.

**Feeding guide for a Lagotto Romagnolo puppy**

Puppies need to be fed a highly nutritious, good quality diet for them to develop and grow as they should. As a rough guide, a Lagotto puppy can be fed the following amounts every day making sure their meals are evenly spread out throughout the day and it's best to feed them 3 or 4 times a day:

- 2 months old - 140 g to 208 g depending on a puppy's build
- 3 months old - 166 g to 246 g depending on a puppy's build
- 4 months old - 177 g to 264 g depending on a puppy's build
- 6 months old - 179 g to 270 g depending on a puppy's build
- 7 months old - 161 g to 250 g depending on a puppy's build
- 8 months old - 143 g to 233 g depending on a puppy's build
- 10 months old - 126 g to 194 g depending on a puppy's build
- 11 months old - 124 g to 192 g depending on a puppy's build
- Once a puppy is 12 months old they can be fed adult dog food.

**Feeding guide for an adult Lagotto Romagnolo**

Once fully mature, an adult Lagotto Romagnolo must be fed a good quality diet to ensure their continued good health. As a rough guide, an adult Lagotto can be fed the following amounts every day:

- Dogs weighing 11 kg can be fed 148g to 194g depending on activity
- Dogs weighing 13 kg can be fed 158g to 208g depending on activity
- Dogs weighing 14 kg can be fed 177g to 233g depending on activity
- Dogs weighing 16 kg can be fed 196g to 258g depending on activity

Ingram Content Group UK Ltd.
Milton Keynes UK
UKHW011312220523
422148UK00004B/269

9 798463 505293